Brigadier General Samuel B. Griffith II, USMC: Marine Translator and Interpreter of Chinese Military Thought

Author: Major Peter Y. Ban, USMC

EXECUTIVE SUMMARY

The works of General Griffith provide a framework of understanding for interpreting the actions of leaders of Communist China that remains relevant for the 21st century military professional.

General Griffith was widely regarded as an expert on military matters and on China. He was a highly decorated Marine veteran of the Second World War and one of the key leaders of the elite 1st Marine Raider Battalion. After his retirement from the Marine Corps, he earned a D. Phil in Chinese Military History from Oxford University. Griffith's experience and education made him uniquely qualified to write about Chinese military thought. As China continues to grow and gain power.

Griffith's writings provide a framework of understanding. This book examines eight works by Griffith to formulate that framework. There are five key concepts that make up Griffith's understanding of Chinese military thought. They are: (1) Sun Tzu and Mao Tse-tung are foundational influences on Chinese military thought; (2) war and politics are inseparable, they are overlapping parts of the same spectrum of conflict; (3) ten principles guide Chinese decision-making and actions; (4) China will only fight "just" wars; (5) China seeks its "rightful place" in the world.

Table of Contents

Introduction

Brigadier General Samuel B. Griffith II was a consummate scholar-warrior who produced a body of work relating to China that potentially provides great insight into the decision-making and actions of the leaders of Communist China specifically, but not exclusively, with regard to military matters. This book explores this potential by examining his body of work relating to China. The author reviews four books – Sun Tzu, *Art of War;* Mao Tse-tung, *Mao Tse-tung on Guerilla Warfare; Peking and People's War;* and *The Chinese People's Liberation Army* – and four articles regarding China written or translated by Griffith. These works were chosen because they formulate the framework of Griffith's understanding of Chinese military thought that remains relevant to the 21st century military professional.

Griffith was uniquely qualified to assess China's military thought. He was U.S. Marine who fought with distinction during the Second World War. He simultaneously earned the Purple Heart and the Navy Cross (the second highest U.S. military award) for his actions during the battle for Guadalcanal. He was the Commanding Officer of the famed 1st Raider Battalion, succeeding Colonel Merritt A. Edson. These experiences demonstrated his martial ability and show him to be a consummate warrior. As a Captain, Griffith translated Mao Tse-tung's *Guerilla Warfare* in 1941. After his retirement from the Marine Corps, Griffith attended Oxford University ("the first grandfather ever to be admitted to New College, Oxford as a freshman"[1]) and earned his Doctorate of Philosophy (D.Phil.) in Chinese Military History in 1961. His thesis was a translation of Sun Tzu's *Art of War.* He has authored numerous books, stories, and articles, and has been published in periodicals ranging from *The New Yorker* to *Foreign Affairs.*

These experiences demonstrated his intellect and show him to be a consummate scholar. Griffith spoke with authority on matters relating to both military affairs and China.

Translation: Mao Tse-tung, *Guerilla Warfare* (1941)

Mao Tse-tung published *Guerilla Warfare* in 1937. Griffith published what is most likely the first English translation of the work in the *Marine Corps Gazette* in 1941. The translation was published in two parts in the June[2] and July[3] 1941 issues. It was then republished in 1961 with an introduction. Griffith completed the original translation as a Captain shortly after his return from China. While the translation is a remarkable accomplishment in itself for a junior officer so early in his career, even more remarkable is Griffith's recognition of the significance of the work.

Guerilla Warfare was written at the start of the Second Sino-Japanese War (1937-1945). Though it was written in the context of China's war of resistance against the Japanese and is, to some extent, specific to that conflict, *Guerilla Warfare* can be described as a manual on how to conduct guerilla warfare in general. It is the first comprehensive and systematic exposition of how to conduct guerilla warfare. Mao begins with examining the characteristics of guerilla warfare, discussing how it is to be employed within the larger context of conflict and warfare. He goes on to formulate ways of forming, organizing, equipping, and employing guerilla units. The last part of the work focuses on how to conduct guerilla operations.

Mao acknowledges that guerilla warfare is not, per se, the means to an end. He says that guerilla warfare is not an independent methodology, but rather a part of a larger strategy. In the case of revolutionary warfare, "guerilla operations are a necessary part."[4] This is an important point that can easily be overlooked because of the strong linkage between Mao and guerilla warfare. The emphasis Mao put on guerilla warfare can induce the layman to believe that Mao only advocated guerilla warfare. In fact, Mao notes three types of warfare: positional, mobile, and guerilla. **Positional warfare** is conventional operations conducted by conventional units. The primary purpose of positional warfare is to gain and keep physical areas of operational or strategic value. **Mobile warfare** is the utilization of hit-and-run tactics by conventional units. The goal of mobile warfare is to disrupt enemy operations and deplete enemy resources and personnel through attrition.[5] **Guerilla warfare** is the employment of small units of unconventional forces in the enemy's rear areas to harass and weaken the enemy. Guerilla warfare by itself is never decisive. "Regular forces of primary importance, because it is they who are alone capable of producing the decision. Guerilla warfare assists them in producing this favorable decision."[6]

Mao expanded his ideas on the relationship between guerilla operations and conventional operations in his subsequent writings. Mao postulates three stages of the Second Sino-Japanese War, which he contends will be protracted revolutionary war. In the **first phase** the enemy has the initiative and takes the strategic offensive, while the indigenous forces are strategically defensive. During this phase *mobile warfare* is the primary mode of warfare. The **second phase** is a strategic stalemate in which the enemy consolidates his conquests and the friendly forces prepare for counteroffensives. In this phase, *guerilla warfare* is the primary mode. The **third phase** is when friendly forces execute the counteroffensive. In this final phase, *mobile warfare* is again the primary mode, but *positional warfare* will gain greater significance through the phase. In each phase, the other forms of warfare are executed simultaneously but as supporting efforts. Mao understood that for a significant portion of the conflict guerilla warfare was only supplementary.[7]

What is novel about Mao's analysis of guerilla warfare is the recognition of the crucial importance of an ideological foundation of guerilla warfare of a revolutionary nature. He states that "without a political goal, guerilla warfare must fail."[8] Griffith notes this aspect of Mao's work to be the most salient and persistent. Guerilla warfare as a *tactic and technique* has existed arguably since the earliest intellectual conceptions of warfare, and perhaps since the earliest large scale violent conflicts between groups of people. Certainly examples abound in modern history. Examples Griffith cites include Francis Marion, the "Swamp Fox," a guerilla warrior during the American Revolution; the Spanish effort to expel Napoleon's Grande Armée during the Peninsular War; and the annihilation of the Grande Armée in Russia. Lenin inaugurated the concept of needing a political direction for guerilla warfare.[9] "It is not guerrilla actions which disorganize(sic) the movement, but the weakness of a party which is incapable of taking such actions *under its control*."[10] Mao asserted political objectives as the foundation of guerilla warfare and codified the concept as the central tenet of revolutionary guerilla warfare. The Chinese Communist revolution after the Second World War was ultimately successful under Mao's leadership. The defeat of the Nationalists and the establishment of a Communist state, the People's Republic of China, in 1949 validated Mao's concepts and invested them with authority. When Griffith wrote his introduction in 1961, it was clear Ho Chi Minh and Che Guevara were implementing Mao's guerilla warfare doctrine, and it appeared others were likely to do so.[11]

Translation: Sun Tzu, *The Art of War* (1963)

Griffith's published translation of Sun Tzu's *The Art of War* is a revised version of his doctoral thesis for Oxford University completed in 1960. His is the translation used at the Marine Corps University's Command and Staff College, despite the fact that there are

4

innumerable other translations now published. The best Sinological translations can be pedantic and place heavy emphasis on analyzing philosophical ideologies. Griffith's translation, although now somewhat dated, focuses on the military aspects of the work; this was his intention. The Director of East Asian Studies for the Marine Corps University, Dr. Edward C. O'Dowd, an expert on Chinese military affairs, considers it to be the best translation for students of the actual art of war, i.e., military students.[12]

In his introduction, Griffith discusses the historical context of *The Art of War.* Questions still arise as to whether *The Art of War* was the work of a single individual or a compilation of works by multiple authors. Ultimately, Griffith concedes the inability to make final determinations of this question. He contends, though, that "the originality, the consistent style, and the thematic development suggest that *(The Art of War)...* was written by a singularly imaginative individual who had considerable practical experience in war."[13]

Determining the historical period during which *The Art of War* was written is of greater significance in understanding the impact of the work. Through references in the text to political and economic systems, warfare technologies, and strategic and tactical doctrines, Griffith convincingly narrows the period of composition to 400-320 B.C. This frames the work within the age of the Warring States, which Griffith, in concurrence with contemporary modern Chinese scholars, prescribes as the period 453-221 B.C. The conditions of the Warring States period create a work whose utility can be recognized through the history of modern warfare up to current ideas of warfare.

By the time of the Warring States, war in China had become a professional endeavor. The Chinese states had large standing armies led by professional generals, rather that the sovereign ruler and members of his family as had been the case previously. These armies were well disciplined and were able to execute complex maneuvers on a grand scale through a well defined system of command and control. In more ancient times, when sovereigns ruled over their armies, warfare was whimsical and ritualistic. Wars were considered "military adventures to satisfy a whim, to revenge a slight or insult, or to collect booty."[14] Campaigns were seasonally coordinated, avoiding periods of planting and harvesting and of extreme hot and cold. Battles, strongly influenced by soothsayers, often produced indecisive outcomes. Then during the Warring States period a cogent theory of war appeared. The Warring States was a period of continuing consolidation of power, a process that had begun the previous period called the Spring and Autumn period. As several large states emerged and others disappeared, their survival was dependent on their ability to successfully wage war. As Sun Tzu states, "War is a matter of vital importance to the State; the province of life or death; the road to survival or ruin. It is mandatory that it be thoroughly studied."[15] State sovereigns were ambitious and avaricious with the desire to "'roll up All-under-Heaven like a mat' and 'tie up the four seas in a bag.'"[16] Survival thus required a serious study of warfare.

The Art of War reads like a book of aphorisms. It is structure in a way such that, generally, the reader starts with the strategic, then transitions through the operational, and ends with tactical level considerations of war. One of the key concepts is what B. H. Liddell Hart in his foreword called the indirect approach. This is exemplified in Sun Tzu's exhortation to attack the enemy's strategy. The Marine Corps own venerable text *Warfighting* utilized many of the concepts introduced by Sun Tzu. The *Warfighting* definition of maneuver warfare does not limit it to its obvious spatial connotation. Rather, maneuver warfare creates "a turbulent and rapidly deteriorating situation with which the enemy cannot cope.... maneuver warfare attempts... to penetrated the enemy system and tear it apart."[17] This sounds much like attacking the enemy's strategy. *Warfighting* concepts of surfaces and gaps, avoiding strengths and exploiting weaknesses, also parallels Sun Tzu's simile that the army is like water, which circumvents the high ground and submerges the low.

Peking and People's Wars (1966)

Peking and People's Wars is Griffith's analysis of two statements released by the Chinese Communist Party (CCP) in 1965: "Long Live the Victory of the People's War!" written by Lin Piao; and "Commemorate the Victory Over German Facism! Carry the Struggle Against U.S. Imperialism Through to the End!" written by Lo Jui-ching. The Peking New China News Agency International Service released English text of both statements: Lin's on 2 September 1965 and Lo's on 10 May 1965.[18] Lo's statement has long since been forgotten as he fell in disfavor with Mao, was ousted from power in late 1965, and disappeared from the political scene by December 1965.[19] Lin's statement, on the other hand, strongly influenced U.S. interpretation of Chinese strategy for many years with its exhortations for wars of national liberation. Much of this influence results from Lin's high position in the CCP at the time of the writing and his subsequent rise in power and designation as Mao's successor.[20]

When Lin's statement was published, Griffith noted that Lin was "Vice Chairman of the Central Committee of the CCP, a senior member of the National Defense Council, and acting Chairman of the Political Bureau's important Military Affairs Commission. He speaks with full authority."[21] Lin was a graduate of the famous Whampoa Military Academy, which was established by Sun Yat-sen to train a new cadre of leaders for his revolutionary army. He participated in the Long March, the PLA's 6,000-mile trek through central China. This seminal event solidified the core of the CCP. Lin's military renown was great and he rose through the ranks of the CCP. In September 1955, he was designated one of the ten marshals of the People's Republic of China (PRC).[22] By 1966, Lin was designated Vice-Chairman of the Central Committee and emerged as Mao's second-in-command and successor. He remained at this pinnacle of power until his controversial death in a plane crash in 1971.[23]

As the title suggests, "Long Live the Victory of the People's War!" is purported to celebrate the twentieth anniversary of China's "victory in the great war of resistance against Japan."[24] Griffith dismisses this obvious façade and contends that the true purpose behind the rhetoric is five-fold: to present CCP strategy with regard to "wars of national liberation;" to apply Mao's revolutionary model to the undeveloped countries in Asia, Africa, and Latin America; to foment regional and racial animosities; to attack (rhetorically) the United States; and, to proclaim the CCP as the leader of world revolution.[25] The bulk of Lin's statement is the history of the CCP, albeit the most likely the officially sanctioned version. This recitation of history not only commemorates the anniversary, more importantly it is meant to bolster the legitimacy of the CCP and reinforce Mao's leadership.

The latter part of the statement reveals an enticing, but obscure, view of China's strategic outlook and its intentions. Lin states, "at present, the main battlefield of the fierce struggle between the people of the world on the one side and the U.S. imperialism and its lackeys on the other is the vast area of Asia, Africa, and Latin America."[26] This one sentence encapsulated China's view of the state of the world's political situation. The U.S. was the ultimate evil, dominating the weak-willed and preying on the poor. This vilification can be interpreted, in part, as a way to maintain the revolutionary spirit. China's vision of world revolution drew an analogy using Mao's model for the CCP's revolution, likening Asia, Africa, and Latin America to the rural areas and the U.S. and Western powers to the urban areas. In this situation, the peoples of the former encircle and rise up in revolt against and defeat the latter. Griffith notes, without irony, Lin's declared requirement of revolutionary self-reliance: "Revolution or people's war in any country is the business of the masses in that country and should be carried out primarily by their own efforts; there is no other way."[27] Griffith interprets this as means for China, which had limited resources, to keep its options open, especially in case a revolution turns out poorly.

Griffith laments China's failure to adhere to the Five Principles of Peaceful Coexistence (mutual respect for sovereignty and territorial integrity, mutual nonaggression, mutual nonintervention, mutual benefit and equality, and peaceful coexistence) that it appears to promote so vigorously.[28] Unfortunately, Griffith takes the five principles at face value and does not explore them in the context of Chinese thought. More recent scholarship has framed Chinese conception of peaceful coexistence in a way that reinforces the idea that China actually believes it is adhering to its principles and is not being hypocritical. In China's view, advocating peaceful coexistence does not compel abdication of the use of violence. Because China has clearly and repeatedly stated its desire for peaceful coexistence, it has demonstrated morality and righteousness. Therefore, nations coming into conflict with China can be, and should be, punished for disrupting peaceful coexistence. China also expected socialism to ultimately dominate the world's political systems; that was the natural evolution of political systems. A peaceful environment promotes this natural evolution. Ideologically, Communist China believed that over time their system would inevitably supersede the capitalist system worldwide. Though China advocates peaceful coexistence, revolutionary rhetoric simply acknowledges the ultimate state of international political systems.[29]

The Chinese People's Liberation Army (1967)

The Chinese People's Liberation Army is Griffith's contemporary assessment of China's

military capabilities. When the book was published in 1967, China was in the midst of the

turmoil of the Great Proletarian Cultural Revolution. Mao was still in power and was reasserting

his power with the great purges he called a Cultural Revolution. Also in 1967, China was

preparing to detonate a nuclear fusion device mid-year, just three years after it had become a

nuclear power by detonating its first nuclear fission device in 1964. The U.S., on the other hand,

was heavily involved in the Vietnam War with no feasible plan to end the war. Considerable

uncertainty existed as to whether China would enter the conflict; after all, China had intervened

in Korea, it had just fought a border war with India in 1962, and it was spewing bellicose rhetoric

as noted above.

Griffith structured his book into two parts. The first is the history of the PLA from its

establishment in 1927 through the Korean War. The second is an assessment of the PLA's

capabilities, examining military policies, structure, and future trajectory. A fair assessment of

the book would echo Alice Langley Hsieh's review for the RAND Corporation, which opines

that while "General Griffith's study is a useful introduction to the history of the PLA…. The

specialist would have preferred greater attention to such questions as Mao's effort to gain control

of the military in the early thirties."[30] Nonetheless, Griffith provides critical insight into the

Chinese military thought and its relationship to political policy.

Griffith wrote, "The history of the rise to power of the Chinese Communist Party (CCP)

is also the history of the development of the People's Liberation Army (PLA)."[31] This

convergence does not manifest until the Long March, which occurred between October 1934 and

October 1935. The CCP was founded in May 1921, and during the early years it was little more that an academic group. Though the CCP was able to exert considerable influence through the Communists in the Kuomintang's National Revolutionary Army, "the CCP, although ostensibly strong, did not control an instrument of power: an army."[32] This instrument of power was established by a coup in Nanch'ang by four Communist officers of the National Revolutionary Army on 1 August 1927 (among the four were two future great leaders within the CCP, Chu Teh and Chou En-Lai). Unfortunately, Griffith makes only passing reference to General Chiang Kai-shek's purge of the Communists from the Kuomintang in April 1927. This incident split the left and right wings of the Kuomintang and set the stage for the Nanch'ang insurrection. Although the insurrection itself was a failure, the Communists had severed their ties to the Kuomintang Nationalists but gained control of an army.[33]

The Long March enabled the Communists to escape complete destruction and galvanized the CCP leadership. For the Fifth Extermination Campaign (the previous four having been failures), the Kuomintang developed a strategy of mutually supporting blockhouses that was able to contain and defeat the Communists systematically. The Communists, acceding to this strategy of positional warfare, could not contend with the Nationalists' advantage in matériel. It became clear that they would have to abandon their base in Kiangsi, leave the south, and find a safe haven elsewhere in order to survive and consolidate their forces. Thus commenced on October 1934 the year long, 6,000 mile trek west and north, ultimately arriving Shensi in October 1935. Of the 100,000 people that started the trek, only about 20,000 reached the final destination. One of the most significant events during the Long March was the Tsunyi Conference of the Party's Central Committee in January 1935. Griffith states that during this conference, "Mao mustered enough support to gain the unchallengeable position which is still his…. a new leadership was set up with Mao Tse-tung at its head."[34] More recent scholarship contends that, in fact, the CCP did not undergo a significant change in leadership and "Mao was only promoted from a Politburo member to a member of the Secretariat."[35] Nevertheless, the significance of the Tsunyi Conference is in the emergence of Mao as a prominent CCP leader. Ultimately, the Tsunyi Conference and the Long March would define CCP leadership for the next 50 years.

As Mao rose to power, his concepts of revolutionary war came to pervade CCP thought and would develop into doctrine. It is in this light that CCP history aligns with PLA history. As Mao wrote, "Party organizational work and mass work are directly linked with armed struggle; there is not and cannot be, any Party work or mass work that is isolated and stands by itself.... Every Communist must grasp the truth, 'Political power grows out of the barrel of a gun.' Our principle is that the Party commands the gun, and the gun must never be allowed to command the Party."[36] As such, the PLA was the primary "mechanism for agitation, organization, and control of the masses."[37] In order for the Party to maintain control of the PLA, 40% of PLA training time was dedicated to political training.[38]

Another key element of control of the PLA is in its structure. Within the PLA there are two intertwined chains of command. One is the usual military chain of command found in most militaries of the world. The other is the political chain of command that has a political officer assigned to every unit at every level of the chain of command down to the company level. The political leader is of paramount importance as he is the heart of the unit. Leadership and decision-making is accomplished by committee, the Party Committee, at each level of command. The Party Committee usually consisted of the political officer, the commander, the deputy commander, and one or two other Communists. As Griffith emphasized, "Literally nothing could be undertaken in any unit without explicit approval of the Party Committee."[39] The nature and extent of this parallel political structure in the PLA must be understood to acquire a proper perspective on Communist Chinese military capabilities under the burden of party-army relations.

While the PLA at its inception was a professional army, its roots are firmly fixed in its history as a guerilla army, its soldiers recruited from the peasant masses. After the Communist victory, this guerilla army had to transition from a revolutionary force to one tasked with safeguarding national interests, maintaining internal security, and confronting external threats. During this transition the basic structure remained and appears to remain today. The structure results from Mao's dictum, "all guerilla units must have political and military leadership."[40]

Other Writings on China

Besides the four books mentioned above, Griffith wrote extensively about China throughout his life. These range from an article in the *Marine Corps Gazette* that records Griffith's observations while working as a military analyst with the Naval Attaché in Pei-p'ing in 1937 to an unpublished new introduction to his translation of Mao's *Guerilla Warfare,* written some time after Mao's death in 1976. Though, Griffith cannot be described as prolific, his body of work is evidence of his substantial efforts to understand Chinese military thought. This paper examines four essays in which Griffith attempted to make contemporary assessments of Communist Chinese military thought and capabilities. These will be introduced chronologically because they, in fact, can be comprehended better in sequence.

Griffith published "Some Chinese Thoughts on War" in the April 1961 issue of the *Marine Corps Gazette.* Although at that point, China had not entered the nuclear club, it had demonstrated that it was a world power that could not be ignored and this reality had to be accepted. As with all Communist regimes, China cloaked all its actions. Tremendous efforts

13

were made to discover and analyze China's military capabilities, but there was a noted lack of analysis of Chinese military doctrine. Griffith wrote his article to help shed light on the subject. The Chinese have had a robust martial tradition that can be traced back to Sun Tzu, but contemporary Western pundits had a rather poor opinion of Chinese military capabilities (and arguable still do). Of course, that assessment was justified due to the huge industrial and technological gap, but Griffith cautioned against complacency.

Griffith proposed ten principles that guide Chinese actions: morale, deception, surprise, mobility, timing, disruption, flexibility, concentration, momentum, and freedom of action.[41] Although many of these are self-explanatory, a few have distinctly Chinese conceptualizations that require comment. *Morale* refers to the Confucian concepts of proper relationship between, for example, sovereign and subject. It incorporates ideas such as benevolence, righteousness, and responsibility. An important corollary is that a righteous sovereign only involves the state in just wars. *Disruption* includes disrupting the enemy's plans, orient-observe-decide-act (OODA) loop, and alliances. The intent is to create internal strife among the enemy. *Concentration* refers to focusing combat power on a weak point. *Freedom of action* is akin to initiative, but does not necessarily connote offensive actions only.[42] The 21st century U.S. Marine would be familiar with many of these principles as elements of the Marine Corps doctrine of maneuver warfare.

Griffith's second article titled "The Glorious Military Thought of Comrade Mao Tse-Tung," published in *Foreign Affairs* in 1964, reinforces a key element of the PLA.[43] That is the pervasive political nature of the military as established by the CCP. Mao recorded his concept of the military's political responsibilities in 1929, stating that military affairs are subordinate to politics, military forces are responsible for carrying out political tasks, and organizationally the military departments are subordinate to political departments. As noted above, these concepts are manifest in the Party Committee structure of the PLA. The PLA must be Red first, before it is expert. This is anathema to the creation of a modern military in the Western tradition. Griffith notes that the dismissal of key PLA leaders is evidence of conflict within the CCP in its endeavor to modernize its military. In order to counter the dangers of military professionalization, revolutionary fervor must be heightened. China must eliminate or significantly mitigate these hindrances to create a truly first-rate modern military.[44] Griffith ends this piece with an observation he also made in "Some Chinese Thoughts on War": "The Chairman has improved on Lenin's plagiarization of Clausewitz to the effect that war is simply politics in a violent form. Mao once stated the relationship this way: Politics is war without bloodshed; war is politics with bloodshed."[45]

In "Communist China's Capacity to Make War," published in *Foreign* Affairs in January 1965, Griffith tried to make a substantive assessment of China's military capabilities. The release of captured Chinese Work Bulletins by the U.S. Government gave experts an opportunity to clarify the state of the PLA at that time. Griffith's concluded that the PLA ground forces maintained a formidable capability to protect the homeland and conduct incursions into neighboring territories, if only by its sheer numbers. The PLA Air Force and Navy capabilities, on the other hand, were pitiful, as they are more heavily dependent on industry and technology than the army.[46] The controlled Communist economy simply did not have the wherewithal to provide for those needs.

More important, though, were Griffith's assessments of the intangible aspects of the PLA. Though there were problems with morale in 1960-61, those problems had been corrected. Griffith stated, "it is not realistic to assume a crisis of morale in the P.L.A. or to entertain the hope that the armed forces, or really significant elements of them, will prove disloyal to the party."[47] This loyalty was maintained by the embedded political machinery, emphasis on political training, and occasional purges. A significant related assessment, however, was the reduced emphasis on political training. In addition to the need to professionalize the PLA, this shift in training resulted from the recognition that junior leaders lacked combat experience and actual military training had to mitigate the effects. Finally, Griffith hints at possible Chinese aspirations. China feels it maintains its righteousness in fighting "just" wars. China's concept of a "just" war can be self-serving in that it may enforce its "rightful" claims on what it views as traditionally or historically Chinese lands. Mao had claimed these lands to include "Bhutan, Sikkim, Nepal, the Ryukyu Islands, Taiwan, Outer Mongolia, Hong Kong, Macao and the former tributary states of Southeast Asia (less Thailand)."[48]

The question of China's aspirations was further developed in an unpublished work by Griffith, "Communist China's Military Challenge." This paper was completed in 1966.[49] Griffith postulated that China sought to regain its "rightful place in the world." An understanding what China sees at its "rightful place" can be deduced by looking back at Chinese history. For much of its past, China had been the predominant regional power. The Chinese characters for "China" in fact translate to Middle or Central Kingdom. China's influence on countries in its periphery is readily apparent in countries such as Korea and Japan. Since the advent of Confucianism, Chinese society and its relationship with other states had been ordered along the strict Confucian hierarchy. So, China sees its "rightful place" as being the predominant regional power at the top of hierarchy with purview over lesser peripheral states. This exalted position is not simply acquired, rather it is bestowed by the Mandate of Heaven so there is a supernatural quality about it. Communist China is no different; it too aspires to be a

16

hegemonic power. As Griffith observed, "An ambition to play *the* leading role in Asian affairs is one Mao shares with the dynasts who preceded him."[50]

China saw, and no doubt continues to see, the U.S. as the primary obstacle standing in the way of its national aspirations. As noted above Lin Piao had just announced China's advocacy of wars of national liberation. Despite this bellicose rant, Griffith noted that China was not in a position militarily and economically to make this a legitimate threat. Griffith tried to temper unfounded concerns of Communist world domination with astute analysis. As he succinctly wrote, "Suffice it to observe that a revolutionary model which worked in one specific set of circumstances (circumstances which, by the way, were all highly favorable and cannot possibly be repeated) will not necessarily work at another time, in another milieu and under basic conditions which bear little more than superficial resemblance to those existing in China between 1927 and 1949."[51] Mao in fact enumerates these special circumstances in his lecture *On Protracted War.*

Griffith's Understanding of Chinese Military Thought

Griffith never gave a comprehensive description of what he believed to be the key Chinese military thought. A fairly comprehensive assessment of his understanding can be gleaned from the writings that have been reviewed. The foundation of his understanding would be his belief "that Mr. Mao and his comrades are, and will continue to be, Chinese first, and communists second."[52] This is significant in that the way Griffith frames his understanding of Chinese military thought is not particular to Communist China. We can infer that Chinese military thought has threads of commonality running through it over time, despite that fact that it has evolved through the centuries and various regimes. There are five key concepts in Griffith's understanding of Chinese military thought that can be extracted from the writings that have been examined: (1) Sun Tzu and Mao Tse-tung are foundational influences on Chinese military thought; (2) war and politics are inseparable, they are overlapping parts of the same spectrum of conflict; (3) ten principles guide Chinese decision-making and actions; (4) China will only fight "just" wars; (5) China seeks its "rightful place" in the world.

As Griffith notes, "China's martial tradition was born in remote antiquity and has been enriched during almost three thousand years of history."[53] Clearly, two pivotal figures in that martial tradition are Sun Tzu and Mao Tse-tung. For Griffith any appreciation of Chinese military thought must begin with a study of Sun Tzu. Sun Tzu's text is among the Seven Military Classics compiled during the Sung dynasty circa AD 1078 as the official text for military matters.[54] It is further distinguished because it has been the most important military text in Asia for the past two millennia.[55] Arguably, Sun Tzu lays the foundation of Chinese military thought. Similarly, an appreciation of contemporary Chinese military thought must include the study of Mao Tse-tung. Mao builds on Sun Tzu in forming his own ideas of warfare. Griffith stresses that Western leaders should study Mao's speeches and writings, along with their conceptual framework (of which Sun Tzu is one), in order to be better prepared to deal with what has always been an enigmatic country in the Western mind.[56]

One thing that becomes clear from the study of Sun Tzu and Mao is the Chinese view that war and politics are inseparable. Griffith was not convinced that Sun Tzu fully comprehended this idea that war and politics are interdependent.[57] Indeed, Sun Tzu does not explicitly link the two as Clausewitz does with his assertion that "war is merely the continuation of policy by other means."[58] Nevertheless, Sun Tzu at least hints at this relationship when he notes that war is of "vital importance to the State." Mao, on the other hand, is explicit in declaring this interdependence. He reinforces this relationship with his own assertions that guerilla warfare without a political goal is doomed to fail and that the military is the Communist Party's gun. The inseparability of war and politics is epitomized in Mao's conceptual extension of Clausewitz that politics is the continuation of war.

The ten principles Griffith proposes that guide Chinese decision-making and actions are taken out of Sun Tzu's *Art of War* or derived from it. Griffith's intent in proposing these principles was not to present a definitive Chinese doctrine of war, but rather to have a starting point from which Chinese military doctrine can be examined. Although these principles are analogous to principles of war, Griffith asserts they are more comprehensive. As noted, the Chinese believe that war and politics are inseparable and by extension politics is a continuation of war by other means. One consequence of that idea is that these ten principles guide Chinese decision-making and actions in all political situations, whether at war or in peace.[59]

The Chinese concept of "just" wars is difficult to understand, but it must at least be viewed in the light of China's Confucian heritage. Chinese society has been governed by the strict hierarchical principles of Confucius for millennia. Confucian principles define each person's social standing and dictate proper social etiquette and responsibilities based on a person's place in the hierarchy. Conformity equates to virtue and harmonious relations, while deviation equates to moral dissolution. These concepts can be extended to nations. The Five Principles of Peaceful Coexistence is useful in framing what China may consider to be proper relations among nations. A violation of these principles disrupts harmonious relations and is therefore punishable by means of a "just" war. An example of China's idea of a "just" war was its border war with India in late 1962.[60] This war was initiated in response to India's aggressive posture in disputed territories. After China's military forces had soundly defeated India's forces,

19

on 20 November 1962 China unilaterally announced a ceasefire and withdrew. Despite its military victory, China only kept the strategically significant Aksai Chin region and gave up the North East Frontier Agency, which was almost 70% of the disputed territory.[61] Apparently, China really did use its military might to punish its presumptuous neighbor.

China's view of its "rightful place in the world" is less difficult to understand qualitatively, but the bounds of its ambitions are impossible to determine quantitatively. China's rightful place is bound to its traditional belief, backed up by history, that it is the nucleus of world order upon which satellite nations depend for enlightenment and guidance; it is the Middle or Central Kingdom. The Chinese sovereign is endowed with the Mandate of Heaven, a supernatural sanction that bestows legitimacy to the sovereign. The Mandate of Heaven also bestows China's sovereign with superior moral righteousness. This Mandate of Heaven, taken together with the Confucian concept of hierarchical relationships, yields a world order with China near, if not at, the top.[62] Griffith observes that "China's tradition never contemplated an international society composed of nations or states which enjoyed equal sovereign attributes."[63] As China gains power, it may try to reassert its influence over territories that were traditionally under its purview. Whether China's ambitions will be checked by traditional boundaries or whether it will expand its vision of itself as the Central Kingdom cannot be known.

Griffith's Relevance to the 21st Century Military Professional

The relevance of Griffith's work to today's military professional arises from the confluence of several circumstances. Griffith was a consummate military professional and a China expert. China is a rising power poised to challenge the ascendency of the Western world (and especially that of the U.S.). Griffith's understanding of Chinese military thought as outlined above lays a foundation for interpreting China's military and political activities upon which further study can build. The bulk of Griffith's work was done during Maoist Communist China under the umbrella of the Cold War. For the most part, he adroitly avoids the pitfalls of anti-Communist sentiment and distills his understanding of China into its fundamental timeless concepts. The five concepts presented are variously applicable to the three levels of war – tactical, operational, and strategic.

At the tactical and operational levels, two concepts predominate, that of Sun Tzu and Mao being foundational influences and the ten principles. These concepts are not just important for the illumination of Chinese military thought, but for their applicability to an overall appreciation for the art of war. At the tactical level, if demands of time preclude the study of Sun Tzu or Mao, then a thorough understanding of the ten principles will serve the tactical commander well. At the operational level, military planners engaged in the operational art will find useful insight in the writings of Sun Tzu and Mao that will aid the planning process, from framing the problem to the execution of the mission. In fact, leaders at all levels should devote time to the study of Sun Tzu and Mao for their utility in understanding war and conflict, particularly in the context of the current hybrid warfare environment.

At the strategic level, Griffith's concepts provide a framework to help clear away the veil of rhetoric and begin to perceive China's true intentions and aspirations. For Griffith, it is imperative that the U.S. not be complacent in its dealing with China, despite any exaggerations or misgivings about China's military capabilities. "The Chinese have an ability to exist, as a race and a nation, that is simply unparalleled. The empires of Assyria, Babylonia, Persia, Egypt, Greece, Rome, Byzantium, Spain, Austria Hungary – all have gone, all were transitory. All strutted for their little hour or greatness. China has seen them all come and go; she will see others, now waxing mighty, go in their appointed time."[64]

China's rich history inspires in its people a strong sense of nationalism and, with it, a strong desire to be reinstated to its central position. Ultimately, what China wants is to be at least a regional hegemon. China will likely challenge the U.S. in the Pacific, though it may only seek predominance in the South China Sea. China will also likely challenge U.S. presence in Korea and Japan. Historically, though, China has not been a colonial or imperialist power and has never had had an expansionist foreign policy in the colonial or imperial sense. Can it be assumed that China has no design to expand its territory or control other states, with the exception of those it considers to be historically Chinese? If so, it is impossible to sustain this assumption with any confidence.

Griffith predicted that *"when* Mao 'goes' we will probably see entirely unexpected shifts in Chinese domestic and foreign policy lines."[65] This prediction has been validated as we have seen China emerge as having the second largest economy in the world and attempting to take a greater leadership role on the world stage as a means to pursuing its national interests. In the years since Mao's death, the U.S. has struggled to make sense of China's foreign policy as the weight of China's history supersedes the imposed policies of Mao's Communist China. Today we see a very different China that is still trying to sort out the discrepancies between its heritage and its current political structure.

Restoration of power requires a concurrent expansion of military power. If China is to move forward with its global aspirations, it must have a first rate military that can legitimately challenge the U.S. military. There are numerous challenges associated with developing a modern military in the Western tradition. The greatest challenge for China is severe curtailment, or better yet the elimination, of political activities from the day-to-day peaceful administration of its military. Griffith estimates that anywhere from 25%[66] to 40%[67] of training time is devoted to political training or work. This number will have almost certainly gone down since Deng Xiao Ping's reforms in the 1980s, but the Party Committee structure remains. Another concern would be the lack of combat experience. The last major military action the PLA saw was during the Third Indochina War in 1979. Even with a comprehensive training and education program, combat proficiency will initially be lacking in a shooting war.

Communist China continues to be a closed society with very little information available to illuminate its intents and aspirations. In spite of (or perhaps because of) its authoritarian rule, Communist China is emerging out of its status as an underdeveloped country and becoming an economic powerhouse. As its power and influence grow, China will be more assertive in protecting its national interests and fulfilling its aspirations. Although China's interests can be ascertained, its aspirations remain inscrutable. This impenetrability presents is a significant challenge for U.S. policy makers and strategic planners in creating a policy toward China. China is certain to pose increasingly credible challenges to U.S. national interests, but the extent of the threat is unknowable at this time. In acknowledgement of and response to China's growing power, the U.S. has announced a strategic pivot toward East Asia.[68]

As the U.S. refocuses on China, Griffith's work can help leaders to look beyond the rhetoric and make better reasoned assessments of China's actions and intentions. Although continuous study of China is required for a true understanding, Griffith provided a framework that can put context to the actions of this enigmatic nation. This framework is applicable at the tactical, operational, and strategic levels. Though much of the details of his work are now dated, the core of his understanding is indeed relevant to the 21st century.

Appendix A

Career Timeline

6 June 1929	Graduated the U.S. Naval Academy; commissioned Second Lieutenant
1 July 1930	Graduated The Basic School
27 March 1931 – 1 January 1933	Duty with La Guardia Nacional de Nicaragua
9 November 1934	Promoted to First Lieutenant
22 January 1935 – 12 June 1935	10th Marines; participated in Pacific maneuvers aboard USS Utah
19 July 1935 – 9 July 1938	Chinese language student, Marine Detachment, Peiping, China
16 September 1936	Promoted to Captain
2 June 1939 – 28 February 1941	Company Commander, 5th Marines, Quantico, VA, and Guantanamo Bay, Cuba
22 November 1941 – 1 February 1942	Special Naval Observer of British Commandos, London, England
10 January 1942	Promoted to Major
March 1942	1st Marine Raider Battalion, Quantico, VA
June 1942	Sailed for Pacific Theater; Executive Officer, 1st Marine Raider Battalion
7 August 1942	Landed at Tulagi
30 August 1942	Promoted to Lieutenant Colonel
27 September 1942	Wounded at Tulagi
September 1942 – December 1942	Hospitalized
January 1943 – September 1943	Commanding Officer, 1st Raider Battalion
December 1943 – January 1945	Executive Officer and Commanding Officer, Officer Candidates School, Quantico, VA
May 1945 – December 1945	Commanding Officer, 21st Marines, 3d Marine Division, Guam
9 June 1945	Promoted to Colonel
January 1946 – May 1947	Various billets in Tsingtao, China: Provost Marshal, III Amphibious Corps; 7th Fleet Liaison Officer; Assistant Commander, Marine Forces; Commanding Officer, 3d Battalion, 4th Marines, 1st Marine Division
5 July 1947 – 19 June 1950	Student and Instructor, Naval War College, Newport, RI
9 September 1951 – 10 August 1953	Chief of Staff, Fleet Marine Force, Atlantic, Norfolk, VA
March 1954 – February 1956	Staff, Supreme Allied Commander, Europe
1 March 1956	Retired as a Brigadier General

Appendix B

Career Summary[69]

Samuel Blair Griffith II was born on 31 May 1906 in Lewiston, Pennsylvania. He attended the Donaldson School (now Trinity School) in Ilchester, Maryland, and the Arnold School (now Shady Side Academy) in Pittsburgh, Pennsylvania, as well as public schools in Pittsburgh. His father was an electrical engineer and senior executive officer with the Westinghouse Electric Corporation. Both his grandfather and great grandfather attended Harvard and practiced law, so Griffith naturally grew up assuming he would attend Harvard and practice law. That changed when he met his roommate's brother and his friends who were attending the U.S. Naval Academy. He was sufficiently impressed and entered the U.S. Naval Academy in Annapolis, Maryland, in June 1925. During his time at the academy, he fell in love with his future wife and decided to choose the Marine option to avoid going to sea. He graduated on 6 June 1929 with a Bachelor of Science degree in electrical engineering and accepted his commission as a Second Lieutenant in the U.S. Marine Corps that same day. Griffith spent one year at The Basic School at the Philadelphia Navy Yard, and married Belle Gordon Nelson from Hopkinsville, Kentucky. He felt his time at The Basic School was wasted, commenting the school was run like a Boy Scouts camp. Most of the instructors, with the exception of one or two, were mediocre. One of those was the tactics instructor, Captain Merritt A. Edson, who would later become a Marine Corps legend for his actions during the Second World War. Edson had just come from Nicaragua and his experience made an impression on Griffith.

Griffith received orders to Nicaragua after The Basic School. Since his wife was pregnant, his orders were delayed until after the birth of his child. In March 1931, Griffith found himself in Nicaragua as an officer with La Guardia Nacional de Nicaragua participating in operations against the Nationalists called the banditos led by Augusto César Sandino. He spent two years in Nicaragua and was able to bring his wife out after about a year. Demonstrating a penchant for languages, he mastered Spanish well enough to read Mexican novels and poetry and even read Cervantes' *Don Quixote*. Griffith considered his assignment with La Guardia Nacional as the most rewarding one of his career.

Griffith returned to the U.S. in January 1933 and spent the next two and a half years in various billets on the Pacific and Atlantic coasts and as a student in the Advanced Base Defense Weapons Class in Quantico, Virginia. He spent two months with 2d Battalion, 10th Marines, aboard the battleship USS Utah (BB-31) from April to June 1935, during which they participated in one of the first U.S. Fleet Landing Exercises at Midway Island in the Pacific. Griffith landed on Midway Island with a detachment of Marines. During these maneuvers, Griffith received orders to be a Chinese language student at the U.S. embassy in Pei-p'ing (now Beijing), China.

Griffith and his family departed for China in June 1935 and spent three years in there. For the first two years, Griffith was a language student with no other official responsibilities other than spending six hours a day in instruction. He recalled those years with all the romanticism pre-Communist China evokes. With the start of the Second Sino-Japanese War in July 1937, Griffith assumed the duties of a military analyst for the Naval Attaché. This assignment consumed most of his time and his language studies essentially ceased at that point. However, these years in China were extremely influential and initiated a lifelong study of the country.

Griffith then served as a company commander with the 5th Marines and spent about two years in Guantanamo Bay, Cuba, in 1940-1941. In October 1941, Griffith and Captain Wallace

Greene, a future Commandant of the Marine Corps, were selected to go to Britain as special naval observers of the British Commando training. This assignment was cut short due the Japanese attack on Pearl Harbor and Griffith returned to the U.S. in February 1942. After he returned from Britain, his old TBS tactics instructor Lieutenant Colonel Edson, the Commanding Officer of the newly established 1st Raider Battalion, requested for Griffith to be his Executive Officer. Curiously, there is no connection between observing the British Commandos and his assignment to the Raiders. In fact, Captain Greene was assigned as a staff officer upon his return.

The 1st Raider Battalion first mission was an assault on Tulagi in the Solomon Islands. They landed on Tulagi on 7 August 1942 against little resistance and had the island in three days. The battalion was subsequently moved to Guadalcanal and on 12-14 September 1942 made their legendary stand at what is now known as Edson's Ridge. Griffith took command of the battalion on 22 September 1942 when Edson was given command of the 5th Marines. Griffith was wounded at Matanikau, Guadalcanal, on 27 September 1942. He received the Purple Heart and the Navy Cross for his actions that day (see Appendix D). He was sent to New Zealand to recover and returned to the unit in January 1943. Griffith again distinguished himself in combat during the battle for Enogai in New Georgia, 7-10 July 1943, for which he was awarded the Army Distinguished Service Cross. By September 1943, the strain of combat had deteriorated his health so badly that Griffith was sent home to convalesce.

Griffith spent about one year at the Officer Candidates School in Quantico, VA, as the Executive Officer and Commanding Officer of the school. While he was at Quantico, Griffith was also tasked as the senior member of the Tactical Doctrine of Rifle Squad and Rifle Platoon Board. This board was seminal in the reorganization of the infantry table of organization and adoption of the "fire team" concept of organizing combat infantrymen. The fire team is basic unit of organization in combat units; it is the organizational concept that is utilized in the Marine Corps today. Griffith returned to China in January 1946. He served in various billets in Tsingtao, China, during his 18 month tour. He returned to the U.S. to attend the Naval War College in Newport, RI, in July 1947. He stayed on at the college as an instructor until June 1950. Griffith was assigned the Chief of Staff, Fleet Marine Force, Atlantic, Norfolk, VA, from September 1951 to August 1954. His last assignment was on the staff of the Supreme Allied Commander, Europe, where he worked for General Lucian King Truscott, Jr., until his retirement on 1 March 1956. Griffith said General Truscott was a great commander and considered General Truscott his hero while acknowledging the oddity of a Marine General speaking so highly of an Army General. Although he attained the rank of Colonel during active duty, Griffith was retired with the rank of Brigadier General because of his distinguished combat service.

Griffith earned a Doctorate of Philosophy in Chinese Military History from New College, Oxford University, in 1961. He was widely regarded as an expert on Chinese military affairs. When he was not writing, he was in the employ of institution such as The Hoover Institute, Palo Alto, CA, and the Stanford Research Institute, Stanford, CA. Griffith passed away on 27 March 1983.

SECOND LIEUTENANT SAMUEL B. GRIFFITH II, USMC
(1929)

Lieutenant Colonel Griffith, in his hut on Enogai,
preparing his operation order, ca. July-August 1943.

Lieutenant Colonel Griffith, Commanding Officer, 1st Raider Battalion (2d from left), discussing plans for further operations on Bairoko with (l. to r.) Maj Charles L. Banks; Griffith; LtCol Michael Currin; LtCol George Freer, USA; and LtCol Delbert Schultz, USA, (ca. July-August 1943).

Lieutenant Colonel Griffith (Standing, sixth from left) and officers of his 1st Raider Battalion stand in front of one of the big Japanese guns captured on Enogai. (Over for names of officers.)

Colonel Griffith, commanding 3d Battalion, 4th Marines in Tsingtao, with Lieutenant General Allan H. Turnage, Commanding General, Fleet Marine Force, Pacific, on 9 January 1947.

Colonel Samuel B. Griffith II (center), Chief of Staff, FMFLant, briefing (l. to r.) Major General Field Harris, Colonel C. B. Kirk, and Lieutenant General Merwin H. Silverthorn during 2d Marine Division exercise in October 1951.

Colonel Griffith, Chief of Staff, FMFLant, with Major General Field
Harris, former Commanding General, AirFMFLant, at the latter's
retirement on 24 June 1953 at Norfolk, Virginia.

Brigadier General Samuel B. Griffith II, USMC (Ret) with Commandant of the Marine Corps, General Leonard F. Chapman, Jr., USMC, in the Commandant's office at Headquarters Marine Corps, 2 November 1968.

SOUTH PACIFIC FORCE
OF THE UNITED STATES PACIFIC FLEET
HEADQUARTERS OF THE COMMANDER

In the name of the President of the United States, and by direction of the Secretary of the Navy, the Commander South Pacific Area and South Pacific Force takes pleasure in awarding the

PURPLE HEART MEDAL

to

LIEUTENANT COLONEL SAMUEL B. GRIFFITH,
UNITED STATES MARINE CORPS

for injury received as a result of enemy action in the South Pacific Area on September 27, 1942.

W. F. HALSEY,
Admiral, U. S. Navy.

04436
DTP-298-MLD

The President of the United States takes pleasure in presenting the NAVY CROSS to

LIEUTENANT COLONEL SAMUEL B. GRIFFITH, II, USMC.,

for service as set forth in the following

CITATION:

"For extraordinary heroism while leading the First Marine Raider Battalion against enemy Japanese forces in the vicinity of Matanikau, Guadalcanal, Solomon Islands, on September 27, 1942. With the only other field officer of the battalion killed that morning, and with his men greatly outnumbered and almost completely surrounded by the enemy, Lieutenant Colonel Griffith moved forward to a position where he could reconnoiter the ground in front of him, in order to effectively employ the troops and weapons under his command. While on this mission, he was painfully wounded by an enemy sniper bullet. Refusing to relinquish command of his troops or leave them without a field officer to control the situation, he returned to his post and personally directed the movements of the battalion throughout the remainder of the afternoon. Later, when relieved by a superior officer, he was finally evacuated to a hospital. By his outstanding leadership, great personal courage, and utter disregard for his own safety in a desperate situation, he maintained the confidence of his subordinate officers and the morale of his troops who fought valorously throughout the remainder of the day."

For the President,

FRANK KNOX

Secretary of the Navy.

R - Pittsburg, Pennsylvania.

B - Lewistown, Pennsylvania.

HEADQUARTERS, FIRST MARINE RAIDER REGIMENT
IN THE FIELD
c/o FLEET POST OFFICE
SAN FRANCISCO, CALIF.

29 August, 1943.

SUBJECT: Award of Distinguished Service Cross.

TO   :   Commanding General, South Pacific Area, APO 502.

VIA   :   The Commanding General, Fourteenth Army Corps.

1.   Under provisions of AR 600-45, it is recommended that Lieutenant Colonel Samuel B. Griffith II, U. S. Marine Corps, be awarded the Distinguished Service Cross in recognition of his extraordinary heroism in action against Japanese forces at New Georgia Island, British Solomon Islands.

2.   DESCRIPTION OF THE ACT

a. Date - 7 July to 10 July, 1943.
b. Place - Area from Triri to Enogai Point (G 920-637), along west shore of Enogai Inlet.(Cincsopac Photomap New Georgia 1/20,000).
c. Narrative - During the period, 7 - 10 July, 1943, Lt. Colonel Griffith led the First Marine Raider Battalion in attacks on the enemy to gain its objective, the shore battery at Enogai Point. The occupation of this position was accomplished with the minimum loss of life. During the action, the battalion was attacking an entrenched enemy force over rough dense jungle and through swamp. On many occasions, he advanced alone on personal reconnaissance into areas covered by enemy fire. His brilliant leadership and extraordinary heroism inspired his battalion, which had neither food nor water during the preceeding thirty-six hours, to a final assault on enemy positions resulting in the capture of four 140 m.m. naval guns and the destruction of three hundred and fifty of the enemy. His conduct throughout was in the highest traditions of the naval service. The weather was generally fair throughout the action; the visibility very good. The morale of our forces was very high, and the enemy's equally so.

3.   Since the act on which this recommendation is based the service of Lt. Colonel Griffith has been honorable.

4.   This recommendation is based on the personal knowledge of the Commanding Officer, First Marine Raider Regiment. Supporting affidavits of eye witnesses are attached.

5.   Lt. Colonel Samuel B. Griffith's address is Frankfort, Kentucky. Next of kin: Mrs. Belle Nelson Griffith (wife) Frankfort, Kentucky.

CERTIFIED TO BE A TRUE COPY:

J.C. Lippy
1st Lt. USMC

H. B. LIVERSEDGE,
Colonel, U. S. Marine Corps
Commanding.

29 August, 1943.

STATEMENT OF MAJOR GEORGE W. HERRING:

1.   I have read paragraph 2 (c) above relative to the award of the Distinguished Service Cross to Lieutenant Colonel Samuel B. Griffith, USMC, and affirm that all the facts set forth in the above recommendation are true. I personally observed these actions.

CERTIFIED TO BE A TRUE COPY:

G. C. Lepping
1st Lt. U.S.M.C.

GEORGE W. HERRING,
Major, USMC.

17 December, 1943.

GENERAL ORDERS)
          :
NO....... 502)

I.   AWARDS OF THE DISTINGUISHED-SERVICE CROSS:

By direction of the President, under the provisions of the act of Congress approved 9 July 1918 (Bull. 43, WD, 1918), a Distinguished-Service Cross is awarded by the Commanding General, United States Army Forces in the South Pacific Area, to the following-named officer.

SAMUEL B. GRIFFITH, II, Lieutenant Colonel, United States Marine Corps, for extraordinary heroism while leading the attack on an enemy shore battery at Enogai Point, New Georgia, Solomon Islands, from 7 to 10 July 1943. Colonel Griffith frequently went alone on reconnaissance through areas covered by enemy fire as he skillfully led his battalion in its advance through swamp and dense jungle toward the objective. Although his men had been without food or water for thirty-six hours, his brilliant leadership and courage infused them with fresh energy to deliver paralyzing blows in the final assault during which four naval guns were seized and 350 of the enemy were killed. Home address: Frankfort, Kentucky.

By Command of Lieutenant General HARMON:

A. J. BARNETT,
Brigadier General, GSC,
Chief of Staff.

OFFICIAL:

M. B. KENDRICK,
Major, A. G. D.,
Asst. Adj. Gen.

Endnotes

[1] Samuel B. Griffith, "Some Chinese Thoughts on War," *Marine Corps Gazette,* April 1961, 40-42.

[2] Samuel B. Griffith, "Guerilla Warfare in China," *Marine Corps Gazette,* June 1941. Note: This article was incorrectly attributed to Captain *James* B. Griffith; this was corrected in the next issue.

[3] Samuel B. Griffith, "Organization for Guerilla Hostilities in China," *Marine Corps Gazette,* July 1941.

[4] Mao Tse-tung, *Mao Tse-tung on Guerrilla Warfare,* ed. and trans. Samuel B. Griffith (New York: Praeger, 1961), 41.

[5] Mao Tse-tung, "On Protracted War," *Selected Works of Mao Tse-tung,* Vol. 2, May 1938, http://www.marxists.org/reference/archive/mao/selected-works/volume-2/mswv2_09.htm.

[6] Mao, *Mao Tse-tung on Guerrilla Warfare,* 56.

[7] Mao, "On Protracted War."

[8] Mao, *Mao Tse-tung on Guerrilla Warfare,* 43.

[9] Mao, *Mao Tse-tung on Guerrilla Warfare,* 9-11.

[10] Vladimir Ilyich Lenin, "Guerilla Warfare," *Lenin Collected Works*, Vol. 11, (Moscow: Progress Publishers, 1965), 216, http://www.marxists.org/archive/lenin/works/1906/gw/iii.htm#v11pp65-216.

[11] Mao, *Mao Tse-tung on Guerrilla Warfare,* 4-9.

[12] Edward C. O'Dowd, Director of East Asian Studies, Marine Corps University, "Chinese Strategic Thought" elective seminar, Command and Staff College, January 19, 2012.

[13] Samuel B. Griffith, *Sun Tzu: The Art of War* (Oxford: Oxford University Press, 1963), 12.

[14] Griffith, *Sun Tzu: The Art of War,* 8.

[15] Griffith, *Sun Tzu: The Art of War,* 63.

[16] Griffith, *Sun Tzu: The Art of War,* 25.

[17] Department of the Navy, *Warfighting,* MCDP 1 (Washington DC: Headquarters USMC, 1997), 73.

[18] Samuel B. Griffith, *Peking and People's War* (New York: Frederick A. Praeger Publishers, 1966), 51, 115.

[19] Radio Free Europe Research, "The Origins of the Cultural Revolution: Lo Jui-Ching and the Military Debate," August 23, 1967, http://www.osaarchivum.org/files/holdings/300/8/3/text/11-4-11.shtml.

[20] Samuel B. Griffith, *The Chinese People's Liberation Army* (New York: McGraw-Hill Book Company, 1967), 310.

[21] Griffith, *Peking and People's War,* 11.

[22] Griffith, *The Chinese People's Liberation Army,* 309-310.

[23] Wikipedia, *Lin Biao,* http://en.wikipedia.org/wiki/Lin_Biao.

[24] Griffith, *Peking and People's War,* 51.

[25] Griffith, *Peking and People's War,* 11-12.

[26] Griffith, *Peking and People's War,* 99-100.

[27] Griffith, *Peking and People's War,* 85.

[28] Griffith, *Peking and People's War,* 45.

[29] Chih-Yu Shih, *China's Just World: The Morality of Chinese Foreign Policy* (Lynn Riener Publishers, Boulder, 1993), 42-45.

[30] Alice Langley Hsieh, "Review of The Chinese Communist Army in Action, The Korean War and Its Aftermath, by Alexander L. George, Columbia University Press, New York, 1967; and The Chinese People's Liberation Army, by Samuel B. Griffith, II, McGraw Hill, for the Council on Foreign Relations, New York, 1967," (RAND Corporation, 1967), 3.

[31] Griffith, *The Chinese People's Liberation Army,* 4.

[32] Griffith, *The Chinese People's Liberation Army,* 17.

[33] Griffith, *The Chinese People's Liberation Army,* 17-23.

[34] Griffith, *The Chinese People's Liberation Army,* 51.

[35] Thomas Kampen, *Mao Zedong, Zhou Enlai and the Evolution of the Chinese Communist Leadership* (Copenhagen, Denmark: Nordic Institute of Asian Studies, 2000), 75.

[36] Mao Tse-tung, "Problems of War and Strategy," *Selected Works of Mao Tse-tung,* Vol. 2, November 1938, http://www.marxists.org/reference/archive/mao/selected-works/volume-2/mswv2_12.htm.

[37] Griffith, *The Chinese People's Liberation Army,* 5.

[38] Griffith, *The Chinese People's Liberation Army,* 5.

[39] Griffith, *The Chinese People's Liberation Army,* 254.

[40] Mao, *Mao Tse-tung on Guerrilla Warfare,* 44.

[41] Griffith reiterates these principles of war in his book *The Chinese People's Liberation Army,* pp. 245-248. In his book, though, Griffith uses the word "dislocation" in place of the word "disruption." This author feels dislocation is both less intuitive and less descriptive than disruption and prefers the latter.

[42] Griffith, "Some Chinese Thoughts on War," 40-44.

[43] Samuel B. Griffith, "The Glorious Military Thought of Comrade Mao Tse-Tung," Foreign Affairs, July 1964, 669-674.

[44] Griffith, "The Glorious Military Thought of Comrade Mao Tse-Tung," 669-674.

[45] Griffith, "The Glorious Military Thought of Comrade Mao Tse-Tung," 674.

[46] Samuel B. Griffith, "Communist China's Capacity to Make War," *Foreign Affairs,* January 1965, 236.

[47] Griffith, "Communist China's Capacity to Make War," 231.

[48] Griffith, "Communist China's Capacity to Make War," 222.

[49] Samuel B. Griffith, "Communist China's Military Challenge," 1966.

[50] Griffith, "Communist China's Military Challenge," 4.

[51] Griffith, "Communist China's Military Challenge," 7.

[52] Samuel B. Griffith, "On Understanding China," unpublished, date written unknown, 9.

[53] Griffith, *The Chinese People's Liberation Army,* 207.

[54] Ralph D. Sawyer, *The Seven Military Classics of Ancient China* (New York: Basic Books, 1993), 1-2.

[55] Sawyer, *The Seven Military Classics of Ancient China,* 149.

[56] Griffith, *Sun Tzu: The Art of War,* 55-56.

[57] Samuel B. Griffith, "Sun Tzu and Western Military Thought," unpublished, date written unknown, 14. Griffith writes "I should hesitate to assert that Sun Tzu comprehended the indivisible relationship of war and politics."

[58] Carl von Clausewitz, *On War,* ed. Michael Howard and Peter Paret, trans. Michael Howard and Peter Paret (New York: Alfred A. Knopf, 1993), 99.

[59] Griffith, "Some Chinese Thoughts on War," 44.

[60] Griffith, "Communist China's Military Challenge," 3-4.

[61] James B. Calvin, "The China-India Border War (1962)," (Unpublished Individual Research Seminar Paper, Marine Corps Command and Staff College, 1984), 78-80.

[62] Griffith, "Communist China's Military Challenge," 1-3.

[63] Griffith, "Communist China's Military Challenge," 1966, 1.

[64] Griffith, "On Understanding China," 8-9.

[65] Samuel B. Griffith, "Mao, China and Asia," unpublished, May 1968, 9.

[66] Griffith, "Communist China's Military Challenge," 11.

[67] Griffith, *The Chinese People's Liberation Army,* 5.

[68] U.S. Department of Defense, *Sustaining U.S. Global Leadership: Priorities for 21st Century Defense,* January 5, 2012.

[69] All biographical data is derived from Oral History Program, USMC History Division, "Oral History of Brigadier General Samuel B. Griffith, II" and the Personal Papers Collection, USMC Archives.

Bibliography

Works of Brigadier Samuel B. Griffith, II

Books

Griffith, Samuel B. *Sun Tzu: The Art of War.* Oxford: Oxford University Press, 1963.

Griffith, Samuel B. *Peking and People's War.* New York: Frederick A. Praeger Publishers, 1966.

Griffith, Samuel B. *The Chinese People's Liberation Army.* New York: McGraw-Hill Book Company, 1967.

Mao Tse-tung, *Mao Tse-tung on Guerrilla Warfare,* ed. and trans. Samuel B. Griffith. New York: Praeger, 1961.

Other Published Works

Griffith, Samuel B. "Some Chinese Thoughts on War," *Marine Corps Gazette,* April 1961.

Griffith, Samuel B. "Guerilla Warfare in China," *Marine Corps Gazette,* June 1941.

Griffith, Samuel B. "That Man Suntzu," *Marine Corps Gazette,* August 1943.

Griffith, Samuel B. "Show of Force," *Marine Corps Gazette,* December 1945.

Griffith, Samuel B. "Action at Enogai: Operations of the First Raider Battalion in the New Georgia Campaign," *Marine Corps Gazette,* March 1944.

Griffith, Samuel B. "Corry's Boys," *Marine Corps Gazette,* May 1949.

Griffith, Samuel B. "Guerilla: Part I," *Marine Corps Gazette,* July 1950.

Griffith, Samuel B. "Guerilla: Part II," *Marine Corps Gazette,* August 1950.

Griffith, Samuel B. "Memories and Impressions: Guadalcanal and Tulage, 1978," *Marine Corps Gazette,* November 1978.

Griffith, Samuel B. "North China, 1937," *Marine Corps Gazette,* December 1938.

Griffith, Samuel B. "Zhukov, Khruschchev and the Red Army," *Marine Corps Gazette,* November 1958.

Griffith, Samuel B. "Organization for Guerilla Hostilities in China," *Marine Corps Gazette,* July 1941.

Griffith, Samuel B. "The Glorious Military Thought of Comrade Mao Tse-Tung," *Foreign Affairs,* July 1964.

Griffith, Samuel B. "Communist China's Capacity to Make War," *Foreign Affairs,* January 1965.

Unpublished Writings
(Author's Note: These writings are all available at the USMC Archives at the General Alfred M. Gray Marine Corps Research Center.)

Griffith, Samuel B. "Communist China's Military Challenge," 1966. There are indications that this paper was published in an August or September 1966 issue of a periodical called DIPLOMAT.

Griffith, Samuel B. "On Understanding China," date written unknown.

Griffith, Samuel B. "Sun Tzu and Western Military Thought," date written unknown.

Griffith, Samuel B. "Mao, China and Asia," May 1968.

Griffith, Samuel B. "Sun Tzu and Western Military Thought," date written unknown.

Griffith, Samuel B. New Introduction to Mao Tse-tung, *Mao Tse-tung on Guerrilla Warfare,* date written unknown.

Griffith, Samuel B. "West Point Address," circa 1962.

Griffith, Samuel B. Untitled Work on Guerilla Warfare, date written unknown.

Primary Sources

Oral History Program, USMC History Division, Breckinridge Hall, Marine Corps University, Marine Corps Base Quantico, VA. "Oral History of Brigadier General Samuel B. Griffith, II."

Personal Papers Collection, USMC Archives, General Alfred M. Gray Marine Corps Research Center, Marine Corps University, Marine Corps Base Quantico, VA. "Brigadier General Samuel B. Griffith, II."

U.S. Department of Defense. *Sustaining U.S. Global Leadership: Priorities for 21st Century Defense,* January 5, 2012.

Secondary Sources

Calvin, James B. "The China-India Border War (1962)." Unpublished Individual Research Seminar Paper, Marine Corps Command and Staff College, 1984.

Clausewitz, Carl von. *On War,* ed. Michael Howard and Peter Paret, trans. Michael Howard and Peter Paret. New York: Alfred A. Knopf, 1993.

Hsieh, Alice Langley. "Review of The Chinese Communist Army in Action, The Korean War and Its Aftermath, by Alexander L. George, Columbia University Press, New York, 1967; and The Chinese People's Liberation Army, by Samuel B. Griffith, II, McGraw Hill, for the Council on Foreign Relations, New York, 1967." RAND Corporation, 1967.

Kampen, Thomas. *Mao Zedong, Zhou Enlai and the Evolution of the Chinese Communist Leadership.* Copenhagen, Denmark: Nordic Institute of Asian Studies, 2000.

Lenin, Vladimir Ilyich. "Guerilla Warfare," *Lenin Collected Works*, Vol. 11. Moscow: Progress Publishers, 1965. http://www.marxists.org/archive/lenin/works/1906/gw/iii.htm#v11pp65-216.

Mao Tse-tung. "On Protracted War," *Selected Works of Mao Tse-tung,* Vol. 2. May 1938. http://www.marxists.org/reference/archive/mao/selected-works/volume-2/mswv2_09.htm.

Mao Tse-tung. "Problems of War and Strategy," *Selected Works of Mao Tse-tung,* Vol. 2. November 1938. http://www.marxists.org/reference/archive/mao/selected-works/volume-2/mswv2_12.htm.

Radio Free Europe Research. "The Origins of the Cultural Revolution: Lo Jui-Ching and the Military Debate." August 23, 1967. http://www.osaarchivum.org/files/holdings/300/8/3/text/11-4-11.shtml.

Sawyer, Ralph D. *The Seven Military Classics of Ancient China.* New York: Basic Books, 1993.

Shih, Chih-Yu. *China's Just World: The Morality of Chinese Foreign Policy.* Lynn Riener Publishers, Boulder, 1993.

United State Marine Corps. *Warfighting,* MCDP 1. Washington DC: Headquarters USMC, 1997.